MEMORIES O

AND

CLEETHORPES TRANSPORT

W. H. LUCAS

TURNTABLE PUBLICATIONS
SHEFFIELD

ISBN 0-902844-24-5

Printed by Crown Press (Keighley) Limited

INTRODUCTION

Having been a tramway enthusiast for as long as I can remember, and having worked on transport as a driver for many years, it has always been one of my ambitions to write an account of the public transport in Grimsby and Cleethorpes, both of the tramways and motor buses, with which I have had a close connection and it is written in the style of my own personal recollections of them.

As a youngster I made friends with many of the staff and, as events turned out, worked with many of them in later years. At the present time there are still many who can recall the heyday of the tram in one form or another and remember them under working conditions, but, the day will come when those with an interest can only observe them either in museums, working or static, or else in photographs. Perhaps I may be forgiven for providing one more book on this subject which I trust any who read in the future will find of interest.

To my mind a town or city street looked "just right" with trams running up and down; our old friends had a personality and a "something" about them, which the replacing Motor bus never had, nor ever will have.

The illustrations included are from several different sources. Some are photographs taken by myself, whilst others are from friends and, where known, are duly credited. For those unknown I extend my thanks to you and trust you will not object to the inclusion of them in the book.

Also I must thank my good friend for kindly giving me access to old records relating to dates and costs of vehicles. For this I am indebted to Mr E. W. Mills, Deputy General Manager, Grimsby & Cleethorpes Transport Department. Last, but by no means least, my thanks to Jean Rusling for coping with the unenviable job of re-typing my notes into a readable manuscript.

Grimsby 1973.   W. H. Lucas

PUBLISHER'S NOTE

Mr W. H. Lucas died in January 1973, shortly after completing the manuscript of this book. He wished to leave some small record of the transport system he knew so well and the Publishers are grateful to Mrs Lucas and family for making it available for publication.

Grimsby Corporation No. 21, the first of the Albions. The conductor is Charlie Cod ("Coddy" to his mates), who was well known by many local people.

(Grimsby Evening Telegraph)

GREAT GRIMSBY STREET TRAMWAYS COMPANY
GRIMSBY CORPORATION TRAMWAYS
CLEETHORPES CORPORATION TRAMWAYS
1879-1937

Let me say that I am one of the many who regretted the decline of tramways and their disappearance throughout the country, save for the Blackpool system and those that are fortunately preserved in museums, the best known one being at Crich, in Derbyshire, where, thanks to the untiring efforts of the members, it is still possible to see and also enjoy riding on a representative selection of tramcars from British and continental systems.

The tram was the mainstay of public transport and has never been surpassed in its ability to move large numbers of people quickly, safely and cheaply under all conditions. Another feature was that with regular maintenance and rebuilding where necessary, they would give good service for up to fifty years. Whereas now many undertakings give a bus a working life of ten to fifteen years and out it goes.

I first came to know our tramway undertaking at a very early age. This was the Great Grimsby Street Tramways Company which was part of the Provincial group. I was soon to make friends with many of the staff and came to know some by name. No doubt they grew tired of seeing me around the depot and at the terminus at Cleethorpes asking questions. Many years later I was given permission by Mr Orme White, who was Manager and Engineer, to visit the depot at Pelham Road whenever I wished to do so; needless to say, I made full use of this invitation to see everything at close quarters.

I was born at Cleethorpes in November 1902, a year after the electrification of the tramways. The horse cars began running in 1880; up to 1901 under the management of Mr Montenero. My own recollections begin from the time when I was able to find my way from Mill Road, where we lived, down to the Kingsway Terminus and back, without getting lost. The horse car period is, of course, from information given to me by friends at the depot and from the company records. The later years of operation are from memory, aided by countless notes I made during those early days "watching trams" as I would answer, when my mother enquired where I had been.

At the Terminus the track merged into a single line stub, with the flower gardens continuing along the Kingsway. This stub held three cars, and is today covered by the extended flower beds. The sound of the car wheels as they ran on to the stub and the "plonk" as the point blade moved back into place remain fixed in my memory.

In those early days the cars were open topped and I would stand and marvel at the way the conductors ran upstairs and unwound the trolley rope dropping it over the side to the driver who would turn the trolley ready for the return journey to Grimsby. He would then fling the rope back again to the conductor, who would give it a quick jerk which wound it round the trolley. At one time there was a notice on the ends of the cars just above the drivers head which read: "Swing the pole this way". When the cars were being top covered, this job was done by means of a bamboo pole carried on two hooks on the side of the car above the truck. There were also a number of points along the route where a pole was hanging from an overhead standard for use in emergencies.

After turning the trolley the driver would remove his driving handles from the controller and put them on the Grimsby end, then release the rear end hand brake causing the handle to spin free when he released the iron peg from the ratchet with his foot.

I would stay at the terminus long enough to see all the cars in use that particular day, noting the missing numbers which would be those in the depot for cleaning, or maintenance.

One of my favourite drivers was Mr George Thomas and one day I plucked up courage to ask him if I could turn his trolley. I was soon to learn that the pull on the trolley springs was too much for a young lad as, after unwinding the rope and passing it to me, he slowly let me take the weight. In no time I was jerked off the ground and suspended in mid-air still clinging to the rope. Of course Mr Thomas had to finish the job.

Unluckily one day I contracted measles and the doctor was sent for. There followed something much more serious than measles, to my way of thinking. He told my mother to burn all my collection of tickets, which he said carried germs, thinking I had picked them from the floors and would not be convinced they were saved from journeys made. Looking back I cannot imagine why I did not collect a further set for later years.

As time went by I found my way to the depot by following the lines down Grimsby Road, until coming to the single track going down Pelham Road. Coming first to the house where the Manager, Mr H. L. White, lived, next was the car shed, and next to that the yard and power station.

What a wonderful sight it all was to me! The overheads and the track fanned out into eight roads in the shed. I stared in amazement at what appeared to my young gaze a very complicated layout of points and wires. I was delighted to find several cars standing on various roads in the shed, some for spares at rush hour, while others were in for repairs. How good it all looked! So much so that I ventured into the depths. On the last road was a row of cars which I had not seen in service on our route. I noted that they had only a handbrake at the driving end and the stairs were wrong way round. The top decks were shorter than the usual cars and there was no roof over the driver's platform. I also noted that they were not fitted with a trolley pole. A puzzling sight for a lad of tender years. Looking further down the shed I could see wooden partitions, which I later discovered were the sliding doors into the paint, body and blacksmith shops. I was soon to learn that little boys had no business in tram sheds, and was told on this and later occasions to "hop it", having to content myself with a general view from the footpath outside.

Great Grimsby Street Tramways horse car No. 11 at the entrance to
the Old Park Street Depot. This area is now occupied by flats.
(W. E. R. Hallgarth)

Two horse cars in Old Market Place. View is from the Church wall
looking towards the Corn Exchange.   (W. E. R. Hallgarth)

I made enquiries about the "powerless" trams I had observed in the depot and was told that they were some of the old horse trams, which had been kept to use as trailers, behind other cars and I was later to see them in use in Grimsby on football specials. From my vantage point outside the depot I could observe some of the odd operations that took place when moving trams in and around the shed. When coming out of the depot the cars would push their trollies in front of them, guided by a man with a long bamboo pole.

Little did I imagine that in later years I would be given permission to visit the depot whenever I wished, without expecting to be told to "clear off".

From these early observations I came to know every car individually; every one was different and no two cars sounded exactly alike to my ears. Each one had a motor hum or whine all of its own, whilst the ring of a car's wheels had the same effect. I soon became able to identify any car by ear, both during the day and at night time, even when there were two or three within hearing distance. As may be expected I had to prove this on more than one occasion to disbelieving friends, and I had to take them out in the town to prove it to their satisfaction. When a car received a truck overhaul it became much easier for it seemed to shout the fact to me. I noted recently while reading a most enjoyable book on the tramways of Reading, that Mr Jordon, the author, could also identify cars by sound in the same way. If he should ever by chance read this, he will, for one, agree that it can be done.

I also began to study and make notes of every car in detail, changes to body and paintwork and the advertisements displayed on and inside the cars. I very soon knew every advertisement and which cars carried them. And there were plenty to memorise, both the enamel plate ones outside and the attractive ones inside, in coloured glass, fitted into the quarter lights on the lower deck, most of them having a second row immediately below, between the window pillars. These were very attractive indeed, especially when the sun shone through them. The paper transparencies which replaced them a few years later were a poor substitute.

Having already said that the tram was the best means of moving crowds safely and quickly, also at very reasonable fares, I think it was a pity that this country did not follow the lead of transport authorities in European countries and retain, modernise and extend tramways, instead of being hell bent on scrapping them, which meant that hundreds of cars with many years of further service in them were scrapped.

Of course we know all the excuses off by heart, having heard them all repeated parrot-like as each system was abandoned. The usual reasons which each concern trotted out in turn usually included: "They are noisy". "They cause congestion". "There is not sufficient room for them in the streets". "If a car fails in service, it stops operations on the whole route".

One would think that trams broke down every five minutes to listen to present-day planners. Also one would imagine that motor

Alexandra Road, Cleethorpes.

Alexandra Road in the days of gas lamps. The approaching horse drawn vehicle seems to be caught in the tram lines.

buses were on sale at Woolworths, their being so much cheaper! What a lot of poppycock it was. Other countries can make trams profitable, and have adapted their cities to take them, instead of making a bugbear of them.

To conclude these sentiments, it goes to prove the old saying that "where there's a will there's a way". I sometimes wonder what in the future we shall be lumbered with, when the folks who favoured the bus once more shout "scrap them".

Let us return to the tram routes in the two towns. Starting from Cleethorpes Terminus, the line ran up to High Cliff and down Alexandra Road, passing the Pier and Pier Gardens on the right, whilst on the left was the Empire Music Hall, later to become a cinema. At this early period the Pier entrance was in the Gardens and crossed the Promenade in the form of a bridge. In later years, the entrance was on the Promenade whilst the Pier itself was cut back to the Concert Hall.

A short distance past this point the line turned left and continued along High Street, before descending Isaac's Hill, bearing right at the bottom and continuing along Grimsby Road.

From the foot of the hill the poles were in the centre position, having been side poles prior to this and span wires in the High Street.

Next came Pelham Road, with the single track and overheads running down to the depot. There was also a cross-over at this point, which the cars used to get on to the up line to Grimsby, the previous ones being at Poplar Road and Alexandra Road. During World War I, a cross-over was placed in High Street, which served for the Terminus after dark, as the flashes from the trolleys could be seen from the sea between High Street and Kingsway.

The tracks passed the Grimsby Town Football Ground, which is in Cleethorpes, making "Town" the only team in Britain to play all its fixtures away from home, then on to Park Street, which is the Borough boundary. The old Horse Car Depot was also situated in Park Street. The depot became a skating rink and, at a later date, a cinema, the Strand, a very popular one too and one was always sure of hearing a good orchestra, under the direction of a well known personality, Joey McCall.

The Strand Cinema survived until World War II, when Hitler's Luftwaffe put an end to it. After it was bombed I had a look round and was surprised to find the old tram lines still in position below the wooden flooring. The site is now occupied by flats. The next point reached was Riby Square, with its entrance roads to the fish docks. Here also it was "All change" for Freeman Street close by on the left, into which points led from both the up and down tracks. One curve faced Cleethorpes and saved passengers changing cars for Cleethorpes when leaving the cinemas and the Prince of Wales Theatre on the special cars provided for them. This old theatre made way for the present A.B.C. Cinema.

From here the line was mainly single track with passing loops, and

10

Grimsby Road, Cleethorpes, looking north in the heydays of the tram before the first world war.

Car No. 4 remained open topped throughout its life.

(Grimsby Borough Library)

continued along Hainton Street, now Hainton Avenue, to the terminus at Welholme Road.

A short distance beyond Riby Square, the railway line was crossed on the level, the tram lines having catch points in both directions as a safeguard. From this point a good view was to be had of the Dock Offices, the ships in trading docks and the Dock Tower away down at Lock Pits. After continuing along Cleethorpes Road to Lock Hill, the track turned left along Victoria Street, with the Saw Mills and timber yards on the right; a contrast with the present day view. Only the Dock Offices remain and a fly-over replaces the level crossing. This was rather late in coming, as the railway traffic has declined considerably during the past fifteen years.

After the timber yards came Marshall's Flour Mill (later Spillers) and now a warehouse. Then on to the Palace Variety Theatre, now used commercially. The Palace is situated at the corner of Freeport Wharf, which leads over the Corporation Bridge to Corporation Road. A few yards over this bridge was the Terminus of the Grimsby and Immingham Tramway, which was railway owned.

On the left, opposite the Palace, was the Central Market, with its clock tower. All this has now disappeared and the area given over to industry. A little further down on the right, the Grimsby Corporation built its depot when it took over the tramways in its Borough, in 1925. Today it houses the motor bus fleet, but most of the depot tram track is still in position. The only other reminder of bygone days is the title on the front of the office block, "Grimsby Corporation Tramways".

Passing further on to the River Head, from where the packet steamers ran between Grimsby and Hull, we come to George Street on the left hand side, around the corner of which the tram track ran, then turned right and carried on up Osborne Street, St Mary's Gate and Bethleham Street to the Old Market Place. Here stood the Corn Exchange, a very familiar landmark itself, which, together with several other buildings in the area, became the victims of the onslaught of progress.

We were told at the time that the Corn Exchange had to be demolished to make more room for traffic in the town, and so down it came to be replaced by a car park and flower beds over much of the Market Place, leaving a not too wide roadway around it in the form of a triangle, the centre being used for the Friday market.

From the Market Place, the track continued up Church Lane, turning right, past the Church of St James, left at the top, and over Deansgate Bridge which crosses the former Great Northern Railway. From here, along the residential Bargate, was single track with passing loops as far as Welholme Road, turning left at this point, the terminus was reached at the People's Park gates. These were very attractive and ornate but have now vanished. The single line section of the tram route was protected by signal lights fixed on the wiring standards between the passing loops, which prevented cars meeting on the single sections, the lights being operated by the trolley heads.

Car No. 39, the first of the eight cars built at Pelham Road Depot.
(Grimsby Borough Library)

Ex-Gosport car at Park Street, outside Clee Park Hotel. As No. 22 it replaced the old 22 with bowed top deck roof.
(Grimsby Borough Library)

On the return journey the track in the Old Market Place was laid on the left hand side and turned right into Victoria Street, which was, as far as George Street, very narrow. The "UP" line was met at George Street. This one-way section was for the electric trams only, and did not apply to other traffic. During horse car days, George Street was not used, as the cars used the entire length of Victoria Street in both directions.

This completes a description of the routes and attention must now turn to the cars. In preparation for the change from horse trams, twenty-four 4-wheel cars were ordered from Dick, Kerr & Co. Limited of Preston. They were mounted on Brill 21E trucks and were double-deck open-toppers, with reversed stairs. Seating was longitudinal in the lower saloon, while swing-over "garden seats" were fitted on the upper deck. The trolley standard was offset to the right (as the cars faced Grimsby) providing a seat for one beside it.

Each car was fitted with outside springs and swivel trolley heads. They also had full canopies with headlamps fixed in the canopy surround on the top deck, whilst the upper deck lighting was provided by one lamp attached to a bracket at each end. The cars were adorned with fancy iron scrollwork and painted green and cream, the fleet number was painted on the centre of the dash and also on the waist panel, enclosed by a garter which bore the parent company's title — The Provincial Tramways Company Limited. The title Great Grimsby Street Tramways appeared on the rocker panels. To complete the livery, the cars were lined out in gold and white on the green, and black and red on the white. Seating capacity was 30 on the lower deck and 26 on the upper deck.

After a time in service some of these cars were fitted with top covers, their numbers being: 2, 3, 5-12, 18-24, whilst numbers: 1, 4, 13-17 remained open-topped to the end, with one exception, No. 14, which was top-covered many years later by Grimsby Corporation, when they took over their section, together with some of the cars. Of those top-covered, all except 23 and 24 had bowed tops with three windows in the lower saloon and four in the upper. All had open balconies with a side curved seat for three. An unusual feature of the top covers was that the saloon was slightly longer than that of the lower deck. The upper deck windows were of the drop type, by means of a strap similar to a railway coach, and a number of these cars had wire mesh safety guards round the end balconies instead of the more usual metal sheeting. Numbers 23 and 24 were fitted with what was known as the "Whites Top Cover" with a clerestory type roof.

The unusual cars I had seen during my early visits to the depot were numbered 25-28 and started life as open-sided cars, with cross bench seats. They were built in Germany, for use on the Alexandra Park Line and, following the closure of that system, they came to Cleethorpes, although when they re-appeared on the streets their appearance was similar to the open toppers supplied by Dick, Kerr and Company Limited.

They were wider and higher than the rest of the fleet, due to the

No. 40, built by the old company as an "Open Tourer", seen here at People's Park gates.   (Grimsby Borough Library)

No. 23, decorated for the Coronation of King George V, 1911.
                              (Grimsby Borough Library)

use of channel irons between the body and truck. As a result of this they did not develop the familiar "hogsback" after years of wear, unlike many of the other cars, which had a pronounced droop towards each end due to the overloading during the 1914-1918 war. The doorways in the lower deck were off-set to the near-side, and swing-over "garden seats" were used on both decks. An additional plate was fitted across the front bumper to prevent them over riding the other cars, which of course were lower. The interior paintwork varied in being all white, lined in red and gold, whereas the other cars had varnished wood. In later years these cars were used only for spare working and extras for football matches and carnivals.

To mention once again the identification of cars by sound, these sounded very different from any of the others, although mounted on similar trucks. Throughout their life they were known as the A.P.s by the tramway staff. Numbers 26 and 28 were in later years fitted for use as rail grinders, and were coupled together. They made their appearance late at night or on Sunday mornings to avoid disruption of normal services. They could, however, be used in service if required. Number 27 was involved in an accident in Victoria Street, while crossing an ungated single railway line which served a saw mill. A railway wagon broke loose and ran back over the road, colliding with the tram, causing extensive damage, with the result that number 27 was completely rebuilt. The bottom deck was reconstructed, retaining only the small centre window with the remainder spaced out and larger than previously. The channel irons had been removed, which made the height the same as the Dick, Kerr cars, and with the increased loading in later years this was to prove a mistake, for the inevitable body sag developed. It was sold as a pavilion for the cricket ground at Tetrey, near Grimsby and stood there complete with top deck for a number of years. After the final closure of the system, several tram bodies could be found in villages to the south of the town.

Two more cars were supplied by Dick, Kerr and Company Ltd and were numbered 29 and 30. These were to the same specification as the 1-24 batch. The surviving horse cars used as trailers were numbered 31, 32, 33, 34. In my very young days it was always thrilling to be able to sit and watch the electric car in front, which was towing us. The two cars seemed to be jumping up and down one behind the other, which was caused by the state of the track. The sandy foundations in some parts of the town were a constant source of trouble and even today in some streets the houses seem to be holding each other up. The method of working with trailers at each end of the system was similar to that adopted in some continental countries. A car pulling a trailer would stop and detach it on the double line, then run forward on to the single line stub and depart. The next car arriving would push the trailer on to the stub, and if required, would couple up and depart. These trailer cars were eventually rebuilt by Dick, Kerr and Company Limited as open-top electric cars, with reversed stairs and full canopies. They lasted to be transferred to Grimsby Corporation, after they took over the Grimsby area and were repainted in the Grimsby livery of maroon and cream.

One of the old Provincial "Boneshakers" outside the King's Arms, Waltham. (Grimsby Evening Telegraph)

The only known photograph of Dick, Kerr's demonstration "model", taken on the occasion of Grimsby Trades Fair, 22nd June 1911.
(Grimsby Borough Library)

An "odd man out" was number 37. This car had been on display when new at a tramway exhibition in 1908, but its early history is obscure. In general appearance it resembled the "bowed top" double deck cars, with minor differences to the upper saloon. Twin head-lamps were fitted on brackets in front of the canopy and were so wired, that when the leading end showed two lights, the rear showed one. The stairs were reversed and the fleet number was painted in small figures for many years.

Car number 39 was a single deck vehicle, the body being rather longer than the double deck cars. A clerestory roof was fitted with a small trolley standard with outside springs, to the left of the driver was a seat for three adults. This car saw little use and was kept mainly for advertisements and illuminations, it had originally been at Southport, being number 13 in that fleet.

The company built several cars at Pelham Road depot, the proto-type being number 39. This car was flat fronted, with direct stairs and an open top. It was fitted with a roof in later years, although the platforms and balconies remained open. Car number 40 was an open touring car with no roof, the trolley being mounted on a very tall standard; its use was confined to the summer months only. Although mounted on the usual truck, the length of the body caused difficulty when turning into George Street and after three seasons it was with-drawn and transferred to the Portsdown and Horndean Tramway, where it was numbered 17.

The Pelham Road design was continued with numbers 35, 36, 40 (2nd), 57-60. Numbers 40 and 60 were built with glazed platforms, but open balconies.

The numbers 41 to 56 were not used on Cleethorpes Company cars and Grimsby Corporation used this series for the cars they purchased from Sunderland. On the abondonment of the Gosport and Fareham tramway system, twelve of their cars were transferred to Cleethorpes. These had been built by Brush Electric, and were open top double-deckers, with direct stairs mounted on Brush A.A. trucks.

For service in Cleethorpes they were numbered 1-3, 22-30. Flat roofed top covers were built at Pelham Road for numbers 2, 3, 27, 30. A cover was built for number 22 but not fitted, as the Cleethorpes Council was soon to take over the Cleethorpes section from Kings-way to Park Street.

When Grimsby Corporation took over their area, they acquired from the Cleethorpes company cars number 4-21 and 31-34; they also bought sixteen second-hand trams from the Sunderland District Tramways Company. These were flat topped double-deckers, built by Brush Electric, with open platforms and balconies, the headlanmps being fitted in the centre of the dash plates below the fleet number. Their livery was changed to maroon and cream, lined out in gold with the company coat of arms on the waist panel. The Corporation's title was painted on the rocker panel and, as already noted, they were given the fleet numbers 41-56.

A few of the old company cars were kept for use as specials and were kept in their green livery, but the headlamps were re-positioned

A Palladium charabanc of the Provincial Bus Company on Cleethorpes promenade. (Grimsby Evening Telegraph)

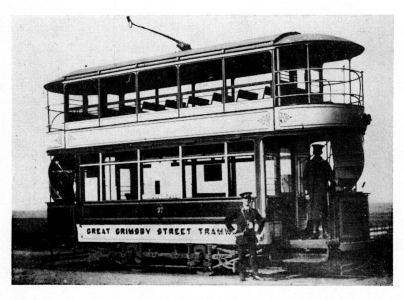

Car No. 37. This was the 1908 exhibition car later purchased by the
company, remaining an "odd man out".

in the dash plate. Whilst some received the maroon and cream livery of Grimsby, numbers 6 and 10 were re-built while still under company ownership and were repainted in their new colours before leaving Pelham Road depot. Number 14, one of the open toppers, was overhauled and given a top cover from one of the scrapped cars and painted in the corporation livery.

The Cleethorpes Company retained numbers 1, 23, 24, 29 from their older cars, but as these numbers had been allocated to four of the ex-Gosport cars, they were re-numbered as follows:

1 re-numbered to 11
23 re-numbered to 18
24 re-numbered to 12
29 re-numbered to 8

All these numbers were vacant, due to the scrapping of Grimsby trams.

From this brief summary of the fleets, it will be realised that the Cleethorpes Council took over an odd mixture of vehicles from the time they held control over their section of the tramways. They also took over two of the ex-Sunderland trams from Grimsby Corporation, when that operator converted to trolley buses. Their numbers were 43 and 47 and both ran in the Grimsby livery during the period of tramway operation in Cleethorpes. The trolley buses and motor buses ran with a blue livery, as did the single deck tram, number 38. This car had the distinction of being the last tram to leave Cleethorpes Terminus on the final night of tramway operation.

The Cleethorpes trams ran under two titles in quick succession, for, soon after the first take over, Cleethorpes became a Borough, the name changing from Cleethorpes Urban District Council to Cleethorpes Corporation Tramways.

Memories of bygone days are brought to mind when some of the fares are considered. Kingsway to People's Park was 2½d, while from Kingsway to Old Market was 2d. There were also penny fares and workmen's returns. In addition, one could buy books of discount coupon tickets at 4½d and 6d. School children's tickets were also on sale in the town's schools and I recall using them when attending school in New Clee during the first world war, our local school being taken over by the army. A transfer ticket was available whereby one could use a Freeman Street car, after leaving the main route at Riby Square.

In 1921, I decided to write to the Manager, Mr H. Orme White, who had succeeded his father, Mr H. L. White, in that capacity, the latter having moved to Gosport to become Manager. I outlined in my letter the interest I had in our local system, and asked for permission to visit the depot and inspect the vehicles at close quarters. This was readily granted along with a letter which I was to produce on the first visit, to whoever was in charge. Needless to say I lost no time in putting in an appearance. On this occasion, the first of many, I met Mr J. Lowis, one of the mechanics. He was one of the staff who in due course came over to Victoria Street at the eventual amalgamation of both Grimsby and Cleethorpes undertakings.

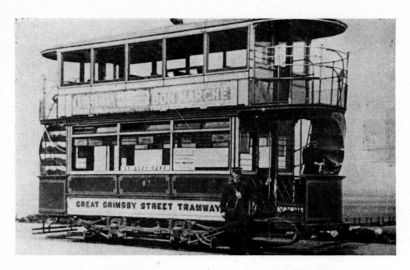

Car No. 6 at Cleethorpes terminus. This was originally an open top vehicle. Note upper saloon is longer than lower.

Car No. 8 (2nd) at Kingsway Terminus. Originally No. 29, this car had a glassed-in canopy. Inspector Clements is standing in front.

On one of these early visits I discovered number 30 at the back of the depot (this was one of the converted "Bull Noses"). It was being dismantled for scrapping and had the top deck suspended from the roof, whilst the lower saloon was being stripped prior to being sawn up for firewood. One of the staff at the depot used the top deck as a tool shed at a nearby allotment.

During this time I made many friends amongst the staff; their names come flooding back over the years and some are still about, living in well-earned retirement. Many local people will remember the names of Thomas, Humberstone, Ravenscroft, Williams, Van der Voord, Clarke, Burgoyne Haines, and Conductor Clarke who once chased me off a tram for going down the front stairs instead of the rear. He still remembers it too! How unpredictable the future is. That day, I little knew he was to become one of my conductors many years later, when I joined the Grimsby Corporation as a driver. I was also able to renew many acquaintances when we all joined forces under the "joint" transport. Two of my school friends were working for the new undertaking. One was the son of Driver Ravenscroft, the other was George Simpson, known to all as "Simmy" without disrespect. Two other well known characters were Sam Wilkinson and Tom Wilson, and familiar figures to older passengers were inspectors Clements, Smart, Roberts, Henley, Willerton and Snow. The latter was destined to become the transport manager at Grimsby.

In concluding the period covered by tramway operation, the following is a list of the important dates in connection with this history. In July 1879, powers were obtained to operate horse tramways in Grimsby and a depot with stables was built in Park Street. Soon after the line was extended towards Cleethorpes. Mr Montenaro was manager at this time. With the advent of electric traction the company decided to change over and began installing the necessary equipment early in 1901. The service commenced on 7th December 1901, the last horse tram operating the previous night. From this date Mr H. L. White took over as Manager, later to be succeeded by his son, Mr H. Orme White, who retained his position until the Cleethorpes section was taken over by the C.U.D.C.

A new depot was built in Pelham Road, for the electric cars; alongside was a generating station for the company's supply. In later years a bus garage was built alongside, between the car shed and Southampton House. This was the manager's residence and office. The Great Grimsby Street Tramways Company operated the whole system until 1925, when, on 6th April, Grimsby Corporation took over the lines in their area. A through service continued to operate and it became common to see red cars in Cleethorpes and green ones in Grimsby. For a short period, until their depot and offices were completed, the Grimsby Corporation Tramways operated from Pelham Road.

Grimsby abandoned the Bargate-Welholme Road section in January 1926, the Bargate section being covered by buses. The Freeman Street route came off next, on 3rd October 1926, the service being replaced by seven single deck Garrett trolley buses, numbered 1-7. At the same time this service was extended to Weelsby Road, where a

No. 27 at Pelham Road Depot, 1903. Note trolley standard mounted on top deck floor.

Car No. 39 at St James' Church in 1935. This was the prototype of eight vehicles, first appearing in open top form.   (M. J. O'Connor)

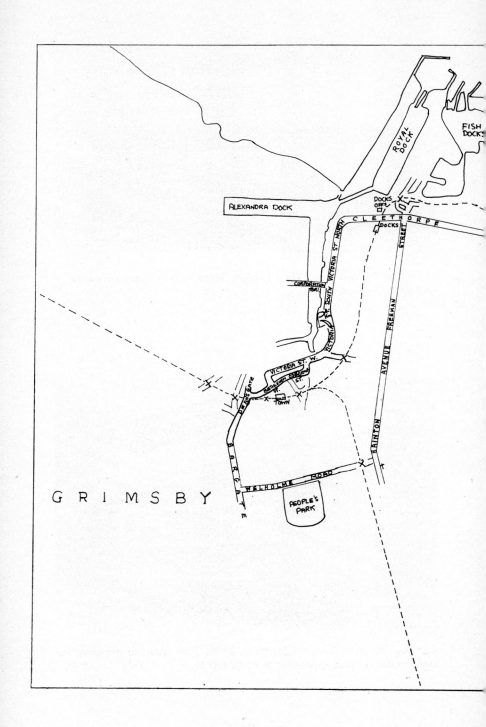

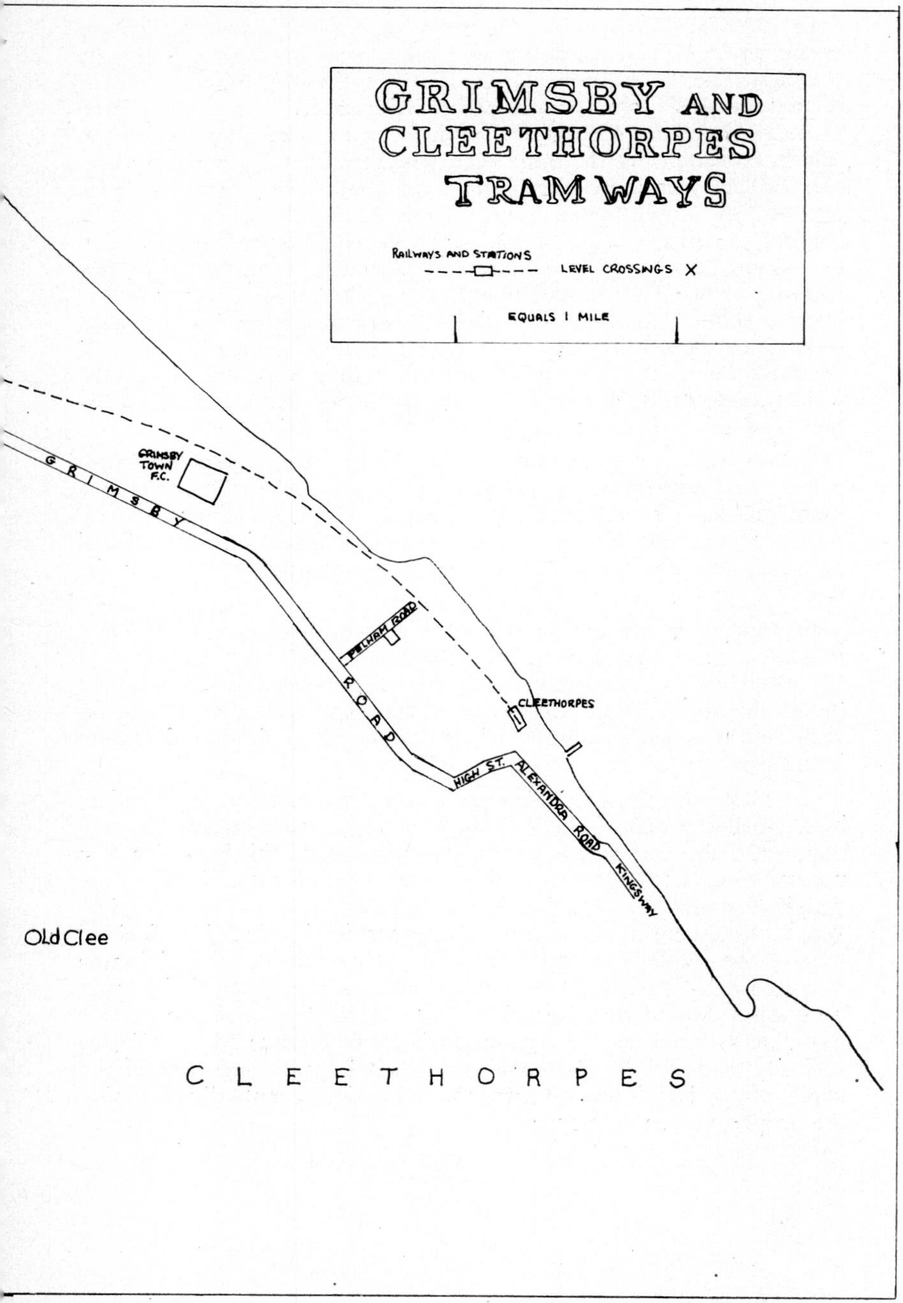

GRIMSBY AND CLEETHORPES TRAMWAYS

RAILWAYS AND STATIONS

LEVEL CROSSINGS X

EQUALS 1 MILE

GRIMSBY

GRIMSBY TOWN F.C.

PELHAM ROAD

ROAD

CLEETHORPES

HIGH ST. ALEXANDRA ROAD KINGSWAY

Old Clee

C L E E T H O R P E S

turning circle was put in. The Company trams at first carried side destination boards, and the Bargate cars carried a large "B" on the front. These were later fitted with end destination boxes.

In 1929 the Gosport and Fareham Tramways closed, and twelve of the cars came to Cleethorpes as replacements for some of the early vehicles. The Cleethorpes Urban District Council took over their section on 2nd July 1936, together with 24 cars, plus two from Grimsby, numbers 43 and 47. Grimsby had ceased tramway operation in November of the same year, when trolley bus operation commenced and continued until 5th June 1960, when they too were replaced by motor buses. Some of the Trolley buses were sold to Walsall and Bradford, the remainder going for scrap. Happily, however, some have survived and are now owned by a number of preservation societies. Cleethorpes U.D.C. (later Corporation) continued to operate trams until 17th July 1937. On the final night the last tram to leave the Kingsway depot was the single deck car number 38. One of those unexplainable events worth recalling was that when the tram was departing for the final journey to the depot it jumped the points on three occasions.

Before turning our attention to the trolley buses and motor buses which took over from the trams, we must include a mention of one more car that visited Pelham Road depot, but on which the general public never rode. So far as I am aware, it made just one official public appearance for it was, in fact, a demonstration car from the builders.

In these more modern days it is the custom of motor bus builders to send a prototype demonstrator around to transport operators to be tested out in service. In tramway days, however, this was not practicable, and so the latest style of tram car had to be placed on view at a tramway exhibition where interested parties could inspect it and place orders accordingly.

To make this business somewhat easier, a number of builders built smaller versions which could be transported with greater ease than a full size car. These were usually about one-third the size of a normal tram. On one of my early visits to the depot I found to my delight that one of these had just arrived and was standing outside. What a little gem it was, complete in every detail. Mr White decided to give the public the opportunity of seeing the model and it was mounted on to one of the company's motor lorries as part of a trade procession around the town. A number of children took the part of passengers, driver and conductor, the latter being dressed in uniforms specially made for the occasion. This model spent some time at the depot, after which it was returned to the builders, eventually becoming the property of an employee.

Grimsby Corporation No. 41 at People's Park gates in 1925. Purchased from Sunderland Tramways.

Car No. 29. Built by Dick, Kerr Ltd, this was originally open topped. Transparent advertisements can be seen below the quarter lights.

TROLLEY AND MOTOR BUS FLEETS OF
THE PROVINCIAL TRAMWAYS COMPANY
GRIMSBY CORPORATION TRANSPORT
CLEETHORPES URBAN DISTRICT COUNCIL
(later Corporation)

The first bus services were operated by the Great Grimsby Tramways Company. During this time they operated the tram services in both Grimsby and Cleethorpes, this concern being one of the companies of the Provincial Tramways Company.

In the days of open tops and solid tyres, they operated routes to Waltham and Caistor. These started from the Corn Exchange, in the Old Market Place, a landmark that has long since vanished. Later, they departed from Brighowgate, at a point opposite the present Bus Station (at which point the present country bus services arrive and depart).

Double and single deck vehicles were used and included such makes as: Commer, Daimler, Palladium, Selden, Garford and Thorneycroft. There was also a Scout chassis on which the tower wagon for the tramway wire maintenance was mounted. This vehicle had a relatively short life, being replaced by a Thorneycroft.

Shortly before the first world war, an experiment was carried out with a steam bus, without a great deal of success. I made several journeys in this vehicle, and well remember the smell of hot oil and fumes which were in evidence inside the bus. Not very enjoyable on a hot summer's day, with a full load of passengers. The body was later fitted to a Palladium chassis and given fleet number 17. The steamer chassis was converted for use as a depot wagon.

A considerable amount of body building and alteration was carried out at the depot in Pelham Road; some of the buses were fitted with new bodies and it became a familiar sight to see posters and bills offering "Obsolete Bus Bodies for sale £5". During the holiday season, the company ran charabanc tours and private hire from Cleethorpes Pier and the Market Place.

The livery of all the vehicles was green and cream, as carried by the trams, with one exception. This was number 25, which was a Clyde, painted in cream and lined out in gold. There was a story that this vehicle was supplied free by the manufacturers and that the company did not want to go to the trouble of repainting it green, in case it offended the makers. A story, I should add, that has never been corroborated. The remainder of the charabanc fleet was made up of vehicles of similar makes to the motor buses, with a variety of canvas and wood roofs. Many of these vehicles had designs which were to be used in the modern motor bus. The Commers had a quadrant gear change on the steering column, while some of the other makers were experimenting with pre-selector gear boxes. One of the early Commer vehicles, number 7 in the fleet, was converted to an electric welding plant for use on the tramway track. The current for the welder was taken from the overhead wire, by means of a clip, which allowed the

Grimsby and Immingham Tramways Car No. 16 on Corporation Road. This was one of the original batch numbered 1 to 16.
(Robert F. Mack)

Grimsby and Immingham car No. 6, one of three purchased from Newcastle and numbered 6, 7 and 8. (Robert F. Mack)

tram trolleys to pass underneath, the return connection being made by attaching a cable to the running rails.

During the 1914-18 war, many of the buses were converted to run on gas due to the petrol shortage. Some vehicles had gas bags fixed on to the roof, while others towed gas generators on two wheel trailers. A number of vehicles were also commandeered for war service. I recall making a journey on number 13, a newly-built Daimler and one of a batch supplied to the company. The following week it was shipped to France, with others from local operators. It never returned to Grimsby, so no doubt number 13 proved to be an unlucky omen.

In the first summer after the war, a special service was introduced along the sea front. This consisted of toastrack runabouts, fitted on Guy and Chevrolet chassis and proved so popular that the service was retained, to become a big attraction for visitors each year. When the bus services were taken over by the Grimsby Corporation, four of these vehicles were retained for a short period, before being sold to private operators in the area. The Corporation acquired more Guy vehicles, when they took over the Ada services, on 1st July 1934. The cost of this was £6,000 and included all the vehicles and running rights. One of the Ada fleet was a 26-seat Reo, which became number 20 in the Corporation fleet. Being the "odd man out" it was withdrawn before the end of 1934.

We must now look at the motor buses operated by the Cleethorpes Urban District Council; also the trolley buses, which replaced the tramways in the Cleethorpes area. The title of the undertaking became Cleethorpes Corporation Transport.

The first motor bus fleet was the usual mixture:- Gilford, Daimler, Leyland Titan, and one Citroen. All of these were fitted with petrol engines. The fleet numbers were as follows: 2, 6, 7 were single-deck, rear entrance Gilfords. Number 3 was a double-deck Leyland Titan, with a rear entrance. 4, 8, 9 were Leyland single-deckers, and number 5 was a 26-seat Citroen. This was later replaced by a second number 5, which, together with number 7, were 26-seat Gilford single-deck vehicles. Four double-deck Daimlers, with rear entrance, were numbered 9-12 (No. 9 replacing the single-deck Leyland bus referred to).

For special use during the summer months, four double-deck Leylands, with open stairs, were purchased from Sheffield. These were numbered 13-16 and the fleet was further augmented by the purchase of two "low bridge" type Daimlers, with utility bodies, being given the numbers 14 and 15. Further batches of double-deck Daimlers were purchased with the "peace time" Willowbrook bodywork. The fleet numbers allotted to this batch were 16-27, all being by this time diesel powered. Two Daimler single-deckers, with front entrance, completed the fleet and were numbeerd 28 and 29.

With the closure of the tramway system in Cleethorpes, on the 17th July 1937, plans were made to operate a service of trolley buses and ten double deck, rear entrance A.E.C. vehicles were obtained, followed quickly by a further three, the whole batch being numbered from 50 to 62. During the second world war, the last four numbers

Pelham Road Depot. Left to right: No. 35 (with frontal damage), No. 24 (2nd) and No. 57. (Grimsby Borough Library)

One of the original Garratt trolley buses purchased by Grimsby Corporation, for use on the Freeman Street route.

were sold to Nottingham Corporation, who, like so many other large operators, were short of buses. This gap in the trolley bus fleet was made up by the purchase of six vehicles fitted with 8ft wide bodies, four of which were B.U.T. vehicles and two by Crossley. They were given the fleet numbers 59-64.

The livery of Cleethorpes Corporation vehicles was dark blue and cream, later becoming grey with blue bands. With the formation of the Grimsby and Cleethorpes Joint Transport undertaking, all the Daimler vehicles numbered from 14-29, along with the trolley buses, were transferred and had 100 added to their previous fleet numbers. The remainder of the Cleethorpes fleet was scrapped, or sold to private operators. Numbers 4 and 8 were sold to a family of travelling showmen.

32-Passenger 30/60 h.p. Albion 'Bus supplied to the Grimsby Corporation.

One of the first buses operated by Grimsby Corporation. These were numbered 21 to 37 and 39 to 41. Several of these were converted to ambulances during the second world war.

A.E.C. No. 38, the first double-deck vehicle to be owned by Grimsby Corporation. After being damaged by air raids during the second world war, it was rebuilt with a utility, rear entrance body.

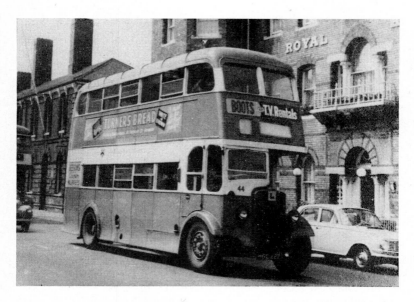

No. 44, one of six vehicles bought from London Transport, on learner duties.

GRIMSBY CORPORATION TRANSPORT
GRIMSBY AND CLEETHORPES JOINT TRANSPORT

Grimsby took over their area of the tramway system in 1925 and for a short time ran the service as then existing. The first difficulty to be encountered was the foundation of the track in Freeman Street and, at a meeting on 5th June 1925, the board was informed that the cost of relaying would be £20,000. The alternative, of converting to trolley bus operation, was given as £12,375 and, as might be expected, the decision to close Freeman Street to trams was taken.

Seven single-deck Garratt trolley buses were purchased, at a cost of £1,475 each. The service commenced on 3rd October 1926, when the route was also extended beyond the original tram terminus, along Hainton Avenue to the junction with Weelsby Road. In 1936 the Freeman Street route was taken over by ten double deck A.E.C. vehicles, with centre entrance bodies, built by Roe's of Leeds. These vehicles were delivered in October 1936 and were given fleet numbers 8-18 (missing out 13). The Garratt vehicles continued in service until 1939, when number 1 was withdrawn. The others followed at intervals, the final vehicle, number 7, being withdrawn in September 1944. The body of number 6 was sold and converted to a seaside caravan, finishing its days at a resort on the south coast.

The trolley bus service was extended when the route between Grimsby Old Market and Park Street (the boundary with Cleethorpes) commenced on 22nd November 1937, the day after the closure of the Cleethorpes tramways. Three utlity-bodied Karrier double-deck trolley buses were bought in 1943, at a cost of £2,980 each. These were numbered 1-3 and were followed by a further batch with standard bodies, numbered 19-24. These vehicles continued to operate until 4th June 1960, when trolley buses were replaced by motor buses, by now operated under the Joint Committee.

The first motor bus service to operate was from Grimsby to Old Clee, about a mile west of Cleethorpes. For this service, six Albion single-deck buses were purchased, in November 1927; these were numbered 21 to 26. A further six were ordered the following year and were allocated the numbers 27 to 32 and in October 1929 five more arrived, to be numbered 33 to 37. The purchase price of these vehicles was £665 for the chassis and £450 for the body, this being supplied by Roe's of Leeds.

As 1926 was the year of the General Strike, it is of interest to recall the effect on the local public transport. On 4th May, no Corporation trams operated in Grimsby, although some motor buses operated between Riby Square and Cleethorpes. Eventually, with the help of volunteers and office staff, a "skeleton" service was managed. Even Mr H. Orme White drove a tram, usually number 3, one of the old brigade and rather worse for wear. It was a difficult period for the staff and passengers and although tickets were issued, many people rode free.

The numbering of buses in the Grimsby Corporation fleet was confusing. Fleet numbers were re-issued from withdrawn vehicles, with the result that high numbers were often older vehicles than low numbers. Some of the Guy utility buses were prefixed "A", although retaining their original number, when withdrawn from passenger service. These vehicles were used around the depot and for staff purposes. The first double deck bus in Grimsby was number 38. This was an A.E.C. centre entrance with a double staircase. During the second world war it was badly damaged during an air raid on the town and was rebuilt with a utility body. Despite its high mileage, 38 worked until after the war, carrying staff to and from Courtauld's factory.

Number 48 was the A.E.C. Q-type, which was delivered in 1934. After a short period on hire to the Corporation, it was purchased for £1,700. It was decided to sell off some of the old Tramway company buses, which had been taken over but not used, to offset the cost of the A.E.C., but the sale raised little more than £260.

The Corporation purchased a variety of second-hand vehicles between the wars and drivers had to be able to adapt to various makes and varying capabilities. From Salford Corporation there came a batch of three single-deck Daimler vehicles, with pre-selector gear boxes and rear entrance bodies. These were allocated fleet numbers 14 to 16. The four petrol engined Guys, taken over from the Ada services, had been given the numbers 16 to 19, but these were withdrawn soon after takeover.

Three more second-hand buses were purchased from Salford in the form of A.E.C. Mark 3 vehicles. These were double-deck, with rear entrances and were numbered 35 to 37. The last vehicle of this batch was soon replaced, when the Corporation bought five Guy double-deck buses from Sunderland, allocating the numbers 37 to 41 to them. These buses were well worn when they arrived at Grimsby and were usually restricted to the "easy routes". Numbers 42 to 47 were six petrol-engined A.E.C. double-deck vehicles, with centre entrance bodies, built by Roe. These were very popular with the drivers, being extremely quiet when running, although by the time I joined the Corporation and drove them they were well past their best. These same fleet numbers were later allocated to six more second-hand vehicles; this time ex-London Transport Green Line. They were A.E.C. double-deck vehicles, fitted with diesel engines.

Numbers 49 to 63 were another series of A.E.C. petrol-engined double-deck vehicles, with the centre entrance bodies built by Roe of Leeds; their styling was later than the batch numbered 42 to 47. A number of this later series were damaged in air raids during the second war, with the result that there was a good deal of repair work carried out, even to the extent of changing bodies. Five of them were actually fitted with new bodies. 55 and 56 received utility bodies with rear entrances, while numbers 60, 61 and 62 were rebuilt with original style bodies. Eventually all these vehicles were fitted with diesel engines. As the earlier vehicles were withdrawn, fleet numbers were passed to whatever batch of vehicles was next purchased. In the case of four ex-Sheffield A.E.C. Mark 3 double-deck buses, these were given numbers 41, 48, 49 and 50. In appearance they were very similar to the London Green line buses and were extremely good

Daimler Charabanc outside the Dolphin Hotel, Cleethorpes. The Provincial Tramways Company operated a number of these vehicles.

Only the bus appears to have changed. Scene outside the Dolphin Hotel in 1967, with the then new No. 37 Daimler single deck for "one man" operation.
(Grimsby and Cleethorpes Joint Transport)

runners. I, for one, was sorry when their turn came for withdrawal.

During the second world war a batch of Utility Guys was delivered and numbered 70 to 79. They were not an easy bus to drive and the cabs were most difficult to get out of. On more than one occasion I have slipped on the step and, on one winter night, actually landed in a heap in the middle of the road. After the war numbers 73 and 78 were re-bodied and fitted with Daimler fluid-flywheel transmission. This gave them a new lease of life, and they remained in service after the others were scrapped. They were, however, re-numbered 114 and 115.

During Mr H. Snow's term of management, further batches of A.E.C. Mark 1 and Mark 3 vehicles arrived. These were all rear entrance bodies, built by Roe of Leeds. The Mark 1 models were numbered 80 to 82, while numbers 83 to 100 were given to the Mark 3 versions. Three A.E.C. Mark 3 buses were purchased from Nottingham, to replace the three numbered 80 to 82 and they were allocated these numbers. Later they were re-numbered 112, 113 and 114 (which was by now vacant again).

Seven A.E.C. buses, with all metal bodies, were bought as replacements for some of the earlier second-hand vehicles, taking the numbers 101 to 107. Only 107 remains and is used as a driving instruction vehicle. More A.E.C. vehicles were acquired, this time the ubiquitous "Bridgemaster" and were numbered 108, 109, 130 to 133. The numbers 110 and 111 were given to two Gardner-engined Daimler buses, with 8ft wide bodies. These vehicles were fitted with ordinary gearboxes.

The buses which came from Cleethorpes when the Joint Transport Committee was formed, had 100 added to their fleet numbers to avoid confusion with those already in use in Grimsby. Numbers 114 to 127 were Daimler rear entrance, fitted with Willowbrook bodies. Later, 114 and 115 had their bodies raised and were similar to the Guy vehicles, numbers 73 and 78.

Number 127 was the last vehicle I drove on my final night of service before retirement and when the time came for its withdrawal from service, I acquired the varnished wooden panels from the top and bottom decks, with fleet numbers and the usual remarks in gold leaf.

Numbers 128 and 129 were also ex-Cleethorpes vehicles. These were also Daimlers, fitted with under-floor engines. Being single-deck with front entrance loading, they were used as one-man operated buses. The largest batch of buses in use is the series numbered 2 to 47. There are, however, four numbers missing, which were the ex-Salford vehicles 14 to 16 and 27. The 42 vehicles are A.E.C. and Daimler, and were ordered in three different batches. The oldest are numbers 25 to 30, while the later batch was from 34 upwards. Number 13 was allocated, unlike earlier buses, which had never carried this superstitious number.

An earlier series, later converted to one-man-operation, were six A.E.C. single-deck vehicles, with rear entrance bodies. Number 68 had been one of the war victims and was re-constructed with a single-deck utility body and a petrol engine. The diesel engine removed was later fitted to number 59, being the first of the old centre entrance A.E.C. buses to be modified.

A re-issue of fleet numbers 51 to 57 was allocated to seven Daimler double deck vehicles. These were fitted with 8ft wide bodies and front entrances. Numbers 58 to 64 were given to a batch of A.E.C. buses of similar styling. Daimler Fleetline buses now make up the second largest batch. These are numbered from 65 to 105 with three variations of bodies and seating arrangements. Number 94 is fitted with a detachable top, which enables the bus to be converted to an open top vehicle, for use during the summer months, along the Cleethorpes Promenade.

One other "odd man out" which deserves a mention, was a single-deck Bristol bus from Rotherham Corporation. This was adapted for the use of people with invalid chairs and was used by the Welfare Department. It retained its Rotherham fleet number of 140 until withdrawal.

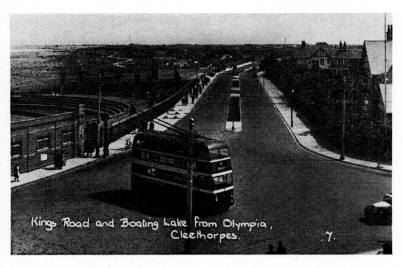

Kings Road and Boating Lake from Olympia, Cleethorpes.

Cleethorpes Corporation trolley bus at the bathing pool turning circle. The livery is dark blue with white bands.

MEMORIES AND ANECDOTES

After considering the motor bus as we know it today, with its superiority over the older types of past years, to say nothing of the increased comfort for passengers and crew, it would be of interest to cast our minds back over the years and recall some of the memories and incidents of those seemingly far-off days.

Today, the modern bus is a much more efficient machine than its predecessors; breakdowns are far fewer than they used to be, while driving is much easier. Pre-selector gears, fluid flywheels, power-assisted steering and the absence of our old enemy, the starting handle, have all helped to achieve this.

Many of my colleagues had public service careers that began long before mine, but since this book is in part my own memories and personal recollections, I will attempt to recall some of the people and describe a few of the older vehicles which I had to "battle" with and the thrills sometimes experienced in connection with them. The instances described and which I will touch upon as they come to mind, include my seven years with the Lincolnshire Road Car Company, before joining the Grimsby Corporation in December 1944.

On joining the Road Car Company, I recall one of the older drivers saying to me, that if I couldn't drive a bus now, I would before the week was out. Although I wondered what he meant, I was soon to find out how true this was. As any older driver will agree, many of the buses, no matter who owned them, were what could only be described as "Hardfaced, stiff steering, temperamental monsters" and it was no easy task to master their varying moods.

At the Cleethorpes depot of the Road Car Company, we were engaged on normal service and contract work, in addition to touring runs at "fourteen miles for a shilling". In the years leading up to the Second World War we had a number of contracts, carrying workmen to the aerodromes being constructed in many parts of Lincolnshire. At the outbreak of war, several of our younger drivers joined the services and, as we became short of drivers, several women were taken on as replacements.

They joined us as drivers of 20-seat vehicles, but very soon tackled the larger 34-seat buses. Two of them I must mention as examples of how we coped with problems during those early days of the "phoney" war. The first has recently been featured in two local newspapers and I know she will not mind my stating that she was disabled. Her name was Kathleen Groome (now Maybury); and if ever a girl showed courage, determination and will-power, she certainly did. Kathleen had to wear special boots, and after mastering a 20-seater, she asked for a test on a larger vehicle. This was turned down but she kept on asking, and was finally given the chance with a 34-seat bus, passing the test first time.

The other girl was Lily Deveraux, who was an unassuming modest type, but a capable driver. One particular day our superintendent asked me to take her for a trial run on one of the workman's services. The vehicle I had was enough for a man to handle, for it was one of

No. 83 of the modern fleet operated by Grimsby and Cleethorpes Transport, on the Bradley route.

A.E.C. No. 61 (JV 5934). This vehicle came to an unlucky end after overturning during the winter of 1962-3.   (Robert F. Mack)

the fearsome Tilling Stevens with the renowned crash-gearbox. Nevertheless she took to it like a duck to water and regularly drove one. Kathleen and Lily were also blackout drivers during the war years.

Mention of the Tilling Stevens recalls an experience I had one winter morning about 6 am. It was I think the closest I ever came to a serious accident and very scaring at the time. It was while working one of the aerodrome contract runs and the bus was full of workmen. On a steep hill the brakes failed completely, and in no time at all we were a "runaway". To attempt to change to a lower gear would have been fatal, as there was little hope of engaging a gear at the speed we were travelling.

At the bottom of the hill were two wartime concrete road blocks which allowed a bus to pass with inches to spare before the road levelled out. By now the vibration in the cab was unbearable, anything that could rattle was being shaken almost to pieces. To this day I cannot remember if my eyes were open or closed as we passed between the huge blocks, but we made it, and I continued to our destination. Needless to say there were some choice words from the passengers, who thought I had done it purposely. As there was no mechanic available that day we had to make the trip home at night without brakes, though none of the workmen knew. There was one big point in favour of the Tillings, they were hard working and were very good hill climbers.

When I joined Grimsby as a driver, I came into contact with many of the men who had driven the trams and heard many tales not normally made public. One such story was told by Roger Burroughs, who had driven trams, trolley buses and motor buses. It happened while he was tram driving and as was the custom at each terminus, the driver or his mate had to change the trolley pole to the other wire in readiness for the return journey. One wet and miserable night, he arrived at Cleethorpes Terminus, and went inside the car out of the rain to talk to the conductor. Time went rather faster than he was aware and suddenly he jumped up calling "it's time we had gone". He grabbed the control handle, rushed to the driving end and was away. Somewhere near High Cliffe he passed a car going to the terminus he had just left. As the two cars passed, the other's lights went out. This amused Roger, for he knew the driver would have to get off and fish about for the trolley pole in the dark and replace it on the overhead wire. At the top of Isaac Hill, a second car was passed on its way to Cleethorpes, and that too was plunged into darkness as its pole was de-wired. Putting it down to coincidence, Roger continued to the foot of the hill, when with a bang and clattering from above all the lights of his car went out and they ground to a halt. From this point the wiring standards were in the centre of the track, and as a result of him having forgotten to turn his trolley pole at the terminus, had been pushing it in front on the wrong wire. On passing the cars whose lights had gone out, he had pushed their trolleys off the wire. Roger surveyed the damage to the overhead wiring from the top deck, and a fine old mess it had made. But he managed to live it down and laughed about it years after.

An even more amusing incident was experienced by another old

Utility Guy No. 71 and centre-entrance A.E.C. No. 51 outside the
depot in 1956.   (Robert F. Mack)

Grimsby and Cleethorpes Daimler No. 127 (ex-Cleethorpes No. 27),
the last bus I drove on the night of retirement.

tram driver. He was about to descend Isaac Hill, when the trolley pole was de-wired and the detachable head was catapulted away. He and his conductor searched everywhere, even in the front gardens of nearby houses. The driver had to appear before the General Manager to explain, and in those far off days there was no union to take up his case. What the boss said was law, like it or not. He was told plainly and simply to go and find the trolley head and not to come back until he had done so.

Two days were spent at the scene where the de-wirement occurred, diligently searching, but no trolley head was found. The third day he was standing once more at the scene, looking at the houses across the road, when he noticed a fair sized hole in a couple of slates. With an inspiration he went and knocked at the door of the house, asking the lady if she was aware of a hole in her roof. He went on to explain and asked if he might be allowed to climb into the false roof. There the search ended, the trolley head was lying on the wooden framework of the ceiling. With this the manager was satisfied and the driver retained his job.

Bus driving has provided many incidents, both amusing and dramatic. Many of them have been passengers with grumbles and complaints, often matched with a witty remark from the conductor. When a passenger asks where can he put his ticket, it requires a great deal of self-control, especially when running late, or full of school children. On the night I fell from one of the old Guy buses, due to ice on the step, a man approached, not in a Samaritan act, but to complain that the service number one had not arrived and did I know the reason for the delay. On the spur of the moment I gave him what I considered a suitable reply, adding that I did not know and cared even less after falling from this "so and so". My conductress laughed for long enough, and when I told her she was about as "................" daft as he was, she laughed all the more.

My memories of the older types of vehicles would not be complete without mention of the Leyland Lioness as distinct from the Lion. My interest in these vehicles began during my service with the Lincolnshire Road Car Company, for we had one at the Cleethorpes depot. It was fitted with a front entrance charabanc body, complete with canvas hood and window frames that folded down when running in fine weather, with the hood down. This vehicle was the last of its type to be in service in Lincolnshire and was numbered 216. The registration number was KO 3420.

My attention was first drawn to this particular vehicle at Cleethorpes, for although fully taxed for service, it was never used. My enquiry to one of the fitters brought the reply that all the drivers refused to have anything to do with it. It was claimed that the steering design made the vehicle dive for the grass on the near-side, or try to ram other vehicles, coming in the opposite direction. The hefty bumper bar at the front certainly bore the signs to substantiate this. Nevertheless there was something about it that appealed to me and I asked for permission to start the engine. It had the usual starting handle and, to use this, one had to stand with the right leg inside the

Alexandra Road and Gardens, Cleethorpes.

Seaside view looking down Alexandra Road. The approaching trolley bus is a 4-wheel A.E.C. of Cleethorpes Corporation, while about to depart is a Grimsby Corporation 6-wheel A.E.C.

bumper, with just enough clearance between the handle and your knees. I was also warned that it had a kick like a mule.

The method of starting was to turn on the petrol and give the engine full choke (this was usually a duster pushed into the air intake on the carburettor). Then the magneto was switched on and the handle turned slowly a couple of times to draw in the petrol mixture. If luck was on your side the engine should start on the next two or three turns. On this particular day I had no difficulty in starting, and after a quick run around the depot yard, was feeling confident enough to ask the Superintendent if I could have the Lioness for use on contract working, as a replacement for the Tilling Stevens I had been using. Despite his warnings that I would regret it, he agreed, and I took over the vehicle until it was recalled to Lincoln depot in 1942. Because of the restrictions on new vehicles, it remained in use, being converted to a wagon body for the maintenance staff. For me it was a sad ending for I had suffered none of the troubles which I had been warned of. The only drawback was the brakes, but this was wartime and we put up with many things which were unavoidable.

During the second war many of the bus concerns were on call to the Army and Air Force, and this included the Lincolnshire Road Car Company. We might be called out at any time of day or night to transport troops who were embarking for overseas posting. One typical journey I recall was when four of us left Binbrook Aerodrome, near Grimsby, in the early hours to ferry some ground crews to Hayling Island, on the Channel coast. The journey took sixteen hours and was very tiring, much of it was during the blackout and our headlamps were masked, save only for the regulation slit of light. After leaving our passengers, we drove the buses into a hanger and wrapped ourselves in blankets, each driver taking the rear seat of his vehicle, and were soon fast asleep. We awoke next morning to the sun shining after a sound sleep, only to be asked if we had found the air raid shelters last night. During the night there had been a heavy air raid on the aerodrome, yet we had all slept through it. We must have been exhausted.

There were many characters on the buses, both passengers and crews, and in the confines of a town like Grimsby both came to know each other by a bond of mutual respect. Unlike many undertakings, which are now motivated by policies often far removed from the basic requirement of serving a public, the Joint Transport Committee of Grimsby and Cleethorpes retains much individuality in fulfilling its purpose to provide the people with public transport.